IMAGES
of America

Presidential Vacations in Florida

On the Cover: The nation's 29th president, Warren G. Harding, relaxes between rounds at his favorite St. Augustine golf course during one of his many vacations to the Sunshine State. (Library of Congress.)

IMAGES
of America

PRESIDENTIAL VACATIONS IN FLORIDA

Robert Buccellato
Foreword by Matthew Algeo

ARCADIA
PUBLISHING

ISBN 978-1-4671-0629-0

Published by Arcadia Publishing
Charleston, South Carolina

Printed in the United States of America

Library of Congress Control Number: 2020947750

For all general information, please contact Arcadia Publishing:
Telephone 843-853-2070
Fax 843-853-0044
E-mail sales@arcadiapublishing.com
For customer service and orders:
Toll-Free 1-888-313-2665

Visit us on the Internet at www.arcadiapublishing.com

To Barry, Miki, and Mom.

Contents

FOREWORD

Some of my favorite pictures of Harry Truman were taken while he was vacationing in Key West. To see him in a Hawaiian shirt, invariably smiling broadly, one can feel the relaxation radiating from the images, offering us, in our current troubled times, a tonic from a bygone era. When Truman visited Florida, he seemed unworried by the enormous responsibilities pressing down upon him.

When the oil magnate Henry Flagler began laying railroad tracks up and down Florida around the turn of the 20th century, he only hoped to attract guests to his resort hotels. But those tracks laid the foundation for what would become the state's most lucrative industry: tourism.

President Taft was an early tourist, riding Flagler's rails from Key West on his way back to Washington after visiting Panama in December 1912. Back in Grandview, Missouri, that December, Harry Truman was 28 years old, single, and living with his parents on their farm, undoubtedly preparing for the long winter to come. Did the young Truman read about Taft's trip in the *Kansas City Star*? Almost certainly. Did he ever imagine that he, as president of the United States, would also visit Key West one day? Probably not.

Florida, of course, has become a presidential election swing state, the winner of its electoral college votes earning an easier path to the White House. So the presidents keep coming to soak up not only the sunshine, but hopefully, a few votes as well.

Some presidents have seemed more comfortable by the sea than others. Kennedy, of course, was nautically inclined. Nixon, who never felt comfortable in anything but a business suit, was not exactly a beach bum, though he accepted the 1968 presidential nomination at the Republican National Convention in Miami Beach.

In a way, Florida has revealed something about the personalities of our presidents. I think again of Truman, a farm boy from Missouri, who found, somewhat incongruously, solace by the sea. Even long after his presidency had ended, until the final years of his life, he kept returning to Key West.

Robert Buccellato has assembled an extraordinary collection of photographs revealing various aspects of the presidency as it relates to Florida. The development of Florida since Henry Flagler built his railroad corresponds with the growth of the American presidency into an institution with prestige and power unparalleled in history. Enjoy these images of people and places important not only to the state of Florida, but to all our United States.

—Matthew Algeo

ACKNOWLEDGMENTS

Thanks, as always, to my wife, Stephanie, and my sons Croston and Noah. Thanks also to my brother Nick and my sister Madison; my grandparents, for those first books on the presidency; my parents, for reminding me of the value of hard work; Anita, "I don't have nothing under that tree"; Roz, for always being encouraging; the Crooms of Crawfordville, who are always helpful; and Red—we miss you.

This book was the creation of many individuals who selflessly searched through mountains of forgotten folders and cabinets to bring these images to you. Some of them were actual witnesses of some of Florida's most historic moments. Specifically, I would like to thank Rep. Walter Young and his wife, Dorothy, and the Florida Museum of History. I would also like to thank the Florida State Archives photo lab, Michael Croom, Jim Williams, Vice Pres. Walter Mondale, and the Jimmy Carter National Historic Site.

Finally, thank you to my project manager and editor at Arcadia, whose guidance made this book possible.

The images in this book are from the Library of Congress (LC) and the author's collection (AC), except where otherwise noted.

Introduction

To define the state of Florida is a difficult task for any historian. It has changed hands among different nations, been the site of defining moments in American history, and decided more than a few presidential elections. The state has grasped the imaginations of countless individuals across every generation. However, despite its national importance, it has never produced a president.

In fact, it has never produced either a presidential or vice-presidential candidate on a national ticket. Rather, it has taken on the form of an adjunct presidential state. From its first territorial governor, Andrew Jackson, going on to ascend to the presidency, to Donald Trump changing his residency to Florida leading up to the 2020 election, the state has had its share of encounters with the commander in chief. It could be because Florida is the "swingiest" of swing states, or it could be its year-round good weather. Regardless, the Sunshine State is the most popular destination for presidential vacations. As long as there has been a modern presidential vacation, Florida has been the site of marathon fishing trips, rounds of golf that vary widely, and more than a few un-presidential Hawaiian shirts.

This book's purpose is to catalog these anecdotes and shed light on Florida's recent ascendancy as a presidential state.

This book is about those wonderfully colorful moments when presidents let the awesome powers of their office melt away and become, momentarily, just another relaxed tourist.

These always ambitious, sometimes brilliant, usually wise, and often entertaining presidents have made their mark on the state.

This is the first book to document all known presidential vacations in Florida, an obscure branch of presidential history, but full of surprises. It is by no means a definitive account of the nearly 200 years of American presidential downtime; instead, it provides a sample of some of the more candid moments in government history.

The connections between Florida and our presidents have created a rich and diverse history with a wealth of exciting events and colorful characters, forming an engaging narrative for any lover of history. The images in this brief book will hopefully add a new chapter to that ongoing story.

One

The President Slept Here

Pres. Woodrow Wilson is pictured in a political cartoon mocking his habit of prolonged vacations. Presidents have faced harsh criticism for as long as they have vacationed. This has led many to get creative in their travel, venturing to places like Florida on official business and squeezing in some relaxation along the way. The American presidency has been linked to the Sunshine State for centuries. (LC.)

It began with Andrew Jackson, eight years before he became the seventh US president. Jackson served as the first territorial governor of Florida for nine months in 1821. He was sworn in at Plaza Ferdinand in Pensacola, and his brief tenure proved eventful, as he used combative methods to settle the native Spaniards and Seminoles. His orders were purposely ambiguous to provide maximum coverage for Pres. James Monroe. (AC.)

Upon leaving office, Pres. Ulysses S. Grant took part in an extensive world tour. It was the first time in the old soldier's life that he had money to burn, and he went to all the best resorts in Europe and the United States. By this time, Florida was becoming a seasonal destination for many well-heeled tourists, and the Grants jumped at the chance to relax in the Florida sun. (LC.)

The first sitting president to visit the state was Chester A. Arthur. Tired of the long Washington winter in April 1883, he decided to take an extended trip across Florida. The itinerary for the official visit took the president and his entourage by fast mail train to Jacksonville, where he was greeted by a large crowd and a reported outbreak of smallpox. (AC.)

President Arthur's trip continued through Winter Park and Orlando to Kissimmee City, where the nation's "Angler in Chief" found excellent fishing. On his first day, he pulled a 10-pound bass from Reedy Creek, today a Disney property, and another 10-pounder the next day. He also sun-burned his face and gained some weight. The trip was cut short after the president started experiencing a mysterious illness. (LC.)

Here is a cartoon showing Chester Arthur and cabinet members, wearing nightcaps, sleeping around a table scattered with papers titled "no ill-will to anyone," and "we need no navy." The cartoon pokes fun at Arthur's lack of energy, which became more pronounced as his health declined. Many believed he contracted the illness that led to his death in November 1886 on the Florida trip. However, he actually suffered from Bright's disease, or nephritis. (LC.)

Toward the end of his life, Pres. Grover Cleveland succeeded Arthur in office. He was just as interested in Florida's mild winters and lovely beaches as his predecessor. Similar to Arthur, Cleveland traveled widely across the state, driving an open carriage through Jacksonville, staying at the finest hotels when visiting Sebastian, and opening exhibitions in Duval County. (LC.)

President Cleveland (right) stands to the side as his successor, William McKinley, is sworn in as president. Despite the rumors that President Arthur's health had been undercut by his Florida vacation, his two immediate successors made trips of their own to the state. Cleveland was warmly received as he explored the Florida panhandle, and McKinley was the first president to make an official visit to the Florida capitol. (LC.)

A massive banquet was held in Pres. Theodore Roosevelt's honor in Jacksonville during his second term. Roosevelt's lasting legacy to Florida was the numerous national parks and preserves he created, such as the Theodore Roosevelt Area at Timucuan Ecological and Historic Preserve near Jacksonville. (State Library and Archives of Florida.)

Pres. William Howard Taft, seen here on vacation, signed Executive Order 1379, creating reserves so that Seminole Native Americans had a place to establish themselves in Southeast Florida. Taft adored Key West and proposed a three-month vacation time for all Americans. (LC.)

From left to right, Thomas Edison, early conservationist John Burroughs, and Henry Ford are pictured at the Edison & Ford Winter Estates in Fort Myers. In 1886, Edison traveled to south Florida and created a winter home he dubbed Seminole Lodge. Several years later, his dear friend Ford bought the adjoining house. Celebrities frequently socialized with US presidents there, from camping with Warren G. Harding to dinner dates with Herbert Hoover. (State Library and Archives of Florida.)

Above, Pres. Warren G. Harding and First Lady Florence Harding (at left) are pictured with Mr. and Mrs. Edward Beale McLean and their son on a pier in Palm Beach. The Hardings made frequent trips to Florida. The first lady suffered from kidney disease, and doctors recommended the couple spend time each year in a warm climate. They traveled with their small circle of friends to both Florida and Bermuda. Before becoming president in 1921, Harding (below) was a frequent visitor to Brevard County. Less than a month before being sworn in, Harding's yacht *Victoria* was stuck for two days as he attempted to sail past Titusville on the way to Merritt Island. (Both, LC.)

Main Street in Jacksonville is seen here around the turn of the 20th century. This city, along with the nearby historic St. Augustine, was a popular destination for the Florida-loving Hardings. As Jacksonville continued to develop as an important East Coast city, it attracted visits from every modern president. (State Library and Archives of Florida.)

The oldest masonry fort in the continental United States, Castillo de San Marcos, is a large Spanish fortress built to defend Spain's claims in the New World. At over 315 years old, it is the oldest structure in St. Augustine and a popular tourist destination. This ancient city and fort have seen many presidential visits. (LC.)

St. Augustine was another favorite Florida town of President Harding. Even before his nomination in 1920, Harding loved St. Augustine and often visited there. After the election in which he defeated James M. Cox and his running mate, Franklin D. Roosevelt, the new Republican president decided to come to St. Augustine to rest and relax and made the nearby Ponce de Leon Hotel his headquarters. (LC.)

The historic Ponce de Leon Hotel, which is now the main building of Flagler College, is pictured here. Like every great hotel, it had a presidential suite and was frequently used by VIP guests. Over nearly eight decades as a hotel, "the Ponce" welcomed a host of notable guests. Among them were five US presidents: Grover Cleveland, Theodore Roosevelt, Warren G. Harding, Calvin Coolidge, and Lyndon B. Johnson. (LC.)

When Harding stayed at the hotel, he would walk every morning along the ancient city's streets. Profoundly popular, he was warmly greeted by everyone he met. Local residents recalled years later that the president-elect was actually given a speeding ticket. The embarrassed officer later stated matter-of-factly, "Well, he was breaking the law, wasn't he?" (AC.)

Pres. Calvin Coolidge was eager to travel once out of office in 1929. Invited numerous times to see sunny Florida, this was his first opportunity to visit as a private citizen, but it came with an obligation: the request to deliver a speech. Coolidge spoke on "The Economics of Life Insurance" at the Vinoy Park Hotel in St. Petersburg. (AC.)

The Coolidges traveled to Silver Springs, Florida, and stayed at Lakeside Inn in Mount Dora, which was managed by their longtime friend Archie Hurlburt. There they spent many happy hours in the main lobby. The first couple walked along the St. Petersburg waterfront and motored to the beaches at Pass-a-Grille in Clement. Reluctantly leaving Florida on February 12, they accidentally forgot Cal's nightshirt at Lakeside. (AC.)

"Woke this morning, looked out of my train window to see palm trees, orange groves, and lovely flowers all around," wrote First Lady Eleanor Roosevelt while taking a much-needed vacation in Florida. "To be transported suddenly into summer was a curious sensation. I had noticed, for the first time, as we came out of Washington, the reddish look on the willow trees, which means that Spring is really at hand." (Franklin D. Roosevelt Presidential Library and Museum.)

First Lady Eleanor Roosevelt is seen here in Miami Beach. Whether meeting with Florida governors, inspecting New Deal work projects, fishing with President Roosevelt, or just answering personal correspondence in the sun, this first lady loved to visit Florida. Long after President Roosevelt's passing in 1945, she continued to make notable appearances as a goodwill guest and keynote speaker across the state. (AC.)

President Roosevelt greets a massive crowd of well-wishers after arriving in Florida aboard a presidential train. He frequently greeted citizens at the back of trains, as he was able to support himself on the railing to help conceal his disability. Even while on vacation, the president's guard was never down. (LC.)

Seen here are images of President Roosevelt in Key West. One of America's most beloved presidents, Roosevelt was almost gunned down in south Florida before his legacy even began. After fishing in Fort Lauderdale and Miami, president-elect Roosevelt was giving a speech at Bayfront Park in Miami on February 15, 1933. Giuseppe Zangara started firing at Roosevelt with a .32-caliber pistol. Although he missed Roosevelt, he shot five other people, including Chicago mayor Anton Cermak, who later died of his wounds. At the time, presidents-elect received little to no US Secret Service protection. As a result of the assassination attempt, President Roosevelt's security was doubled when he traveled. (Both, Rep. Walter Young.)

The legendary Breakers Hotel was founded by Henry Flagler as a premier resort during his Florida railroad expansion. Originally named the Palm Beach Inn, it was a winter hit with wealthy tourists. It became so popular that it was demolished and rebuilt with a larger structure and a new name. This first Breakers Hotel was an impressive 538-room, Italian Renaissance–style hotel that hosted a vast assortment of gilded age celebrities. (LC.)

Pictured here is the Breakers' glamorous south promenade, with its pleasant ocean breezes and filling tea services. Such accommodations, along with a massive renovation in the 1920s, made this a frequent destination for many presidents and presidents-elect. Harry Truman, Gerald Ford, Ronald Reagan, and George H.W. Bush all stayed at the Breakers Palm Beach. (LC.)

This is another view of the Ponce, built by millionaire developer and Standard Oil co-founder Henry M. Flagler and completed in 1888. Today, tour guides take visitors through the structure and regale them with tales of its presidential associations, from Teddy Roosevelt swimming in the nude, Chester A. Arthur fishing for channel bass, Ulysses S. Grant touring the city, and Grover Cleveland being greeted with bouquets from schoolchildren. (AC.)

The Casa Monica Hotel, originally known as the Cordova Hotel, is in St. Augustine. During a recent visit to the city, former president Bill Clinton signed his name on the walls of the hotel lobby. After signing the wall, Clinton took a walk down Aviles Street, where he chatted with tourists until midnight. The hotel later framed the signature in order to preserve it for posterity. (LC.)

President and First Lady Eisenhower watch television in the Breakers' presidential suite. Following the war and several years before winning the presidency, Eisenhower spent time at the former Miami Biltmore Hotel and Country Club in Coral Gables, which was handed over to the US government and turned into a VA hospital. During a more pleasurable trip to Florida, Eisenhower fed the giant turtles at the Key West Aquarium. (AC.)

The Fontainebleau Miami Beach has hosted numerous US presidents, including John F. Kennedy, Lyndon Johnson, Richard Nixon, Gerald Ford, Harry Truman, Jimmy Carter, Ronald Reagan, George H.W. Bush, George W. Bush, and Bill Clinton. The complex's acclaimed restaurants and nightclubs are still a favorite for many former presidents and first families. (LC.)

Seen here is Walt Disney World's legendary Contemporary Resort. Nearly every modern US president has made trips to the happiest place on earth. Nixon attended the Associated Press Managing Editors annual conference here, where he famously proclaimed he was not a crook. Jimmy Carter took his entire family in the 2000s, and the Secret Service used the resort's tunnel system to limit his interaction with the massive crowds. (Rep. Walter Young.)

The Florida governor's mansion in midtown Tallahassee has been the host to several presidents. During the 1980 presidential election, Jimmy Carter spent the night in the mansion's elegant guest room and made the bed before leaving. The Bush family was a frequent fixture during the tenure of Jeb Bush, and mansion staff remember Bill Clinton ordering mango salsa and chips as a midnight snack. (AC.)

Jimmy Carter, known as "the fitness president," is seen here during his daily jog. At the time of his presidency, Carter ran over 40 miles a week. The habit continued into his post–White House life, and he could be seen jogging in the early mornings while vacationing in Florida, with much-younger Secret Service agents struggling to keep up with him. (LC.)

President and First Lady Carter, the ever-thrifty first couple, used their accrued airline miles to finance a large annual family Christmas vacation. The younger Carters usually pick the destination, resulting in frequent trips to the Orlando theme parks. (LC.)

The meeting between Pope John Paul II and President Reagan on September 10, 1987, was the start of the pontiff's eight-city tour of the United States and resulted in some of the largest crowds and traffic jams in Miami history. The two leaders held a private meeting before the pope entered his glass-enclosed car for a nighttime parade on Biscayne Boulevard. (Ronald Reagan Presidential Library.)

President Reagan and Pope John Paul II greet each other at the airport in Miami before their private reception. As many as one million people watched the parade, and an equal number attended an open-air Mass the following day at Miami's Tamiami Park. Catholics from throughout the Southeast made plans to bring busloads of people to witness the first-ever papal visit to Florida. (Ronald Reagan Presidential Library.)

Bill Clinton finishes up a campaign rally in Palm Beach ahead of the 1992 presidential election. The "new Democrat from the South" worked hard to win the Sunshine State, frequently campaigning across Florida. This resulted in Floridians getting to see a lot of him. From running along Tallahassee to eating Latin cuisine in Little Havana, Clinton was the first national Democrat to connect with Floridians in years. (State Library and Archives of Florida.)

President and First Lady Clinton return from another trip to Florida. President Clinton addressed the Florida House of Representatives in 1995, and his visit coincided with the annual Miami-Dade paella day. An enormous paella pan was delivered to the capitol courtyard the evening before the event. The foodie president was at the head of the line to receive his plateful of paella. (William J. Clinton Library and Museum.)

Pres. George W. Bush made numerous visits to Florida to support his brother for reelection in 2002. Democrats had made Jeb Bush their number-one target. The election that year was notable, as it was the first time a Republican was re-elected to the governorship, the costliest campaign in the state's history, and the US Department of Justice sent observers to certain polls. (AC.)

President George W. Bush speaks before a crowd of naval officers at the naval station in Mayport. Since 2000, Bush has been one of the most frequent speakers at political events for Florida Republicans. As a popular president in a critical swing state, his motorcade was a constant frustration in Miami. A competitive sportsman, the state had much to offer the 43rd president in terms of recreation. (LC.)

Here is a closeup of President and First Lady Obamas' hands as they wait to step off a boat in Florida. Such images helped showcase the affectionate nature the first couple displayed in public, which was a refreshing change from the formality of many past presidential couples. Throughout his two terms in office, the Obamas were immensely popular in the state. (LC.)

President and First Lady Obama arrive in Homestead with a Democratic Congressional delegation as guests aboard Air Force One. The favor of riding on Air Force One has been used by many presidents to reward or court politicians of both parties. Since the 1960s, it has been the ultimate show of a Florida senator or congress member's power. (LC.)

President Obama splashes in the ocean with his daughter Sasha. Despite the family's love for Martha's Vineyard as their go-to vacation destination, south Florida had a lot of appeal for the young family. The first presidential family to have young children since the Kennedys, the beaches and resorts of Florida offered the Obamas some much-needed rest and privacy. (LC.)

Pres. Donald J. Trump and First Lady Melania Trump place their hands on their hearts during the national anthem as the Thunderbirds fly overhead before the start of the NASCAR Daytona 500. In the first half of 2020, President Trump made 10 trips to Florida. Each month saw the first family having at least two week-long trips to the Sunshine State. (Photograph by Tia Dufour, courtesy of the White House.)

President Trump arrives at Palm Beach International Airport on his way home to Mar-a-Lago for the weekend. From his first weeks in office, President Trump, like many of his predecessors, has enjoyed getting out of the nation's capital and working from home. Aides have always noted that his mood and energy improve with each visit to Florida. The president usually throws a Super Bowl party at his resort in January, and each March takes part in a tournament at the Trump International Golf Club. Throughout the summer and when Congress is out of session, the president makes public appearances in the West Palm Beach area and holds fundraisers for GOP candidates. On his way back to Washington, DC, President Trump will often stop in Tampa at MacDill Air Force Base to meet with military commanders, receive briefings, and make remarks. (White House.)

Two

No Time to Rest

Andrew Jackson was an accomplished soldier long before he ascended to the presidency. His tours in Florida helped expand his reputation as a military hero in the War of 1812. In 1817, acting as commander of the Army's southern district, Jackson invaded northern Florida, then under Spanish control. After capturing some Spanish ports, he claimed the surrounding land for the United States. Spain protested, to no avail, and despite the following debate, Jackson's actions helped speed up America's official acquisition of Florida in 1821. (LC.)

As secretary of state, John Quincy Adams worked tirelessly to acquire Florida from the Spanish. He then went to great lengths to protect Andrew Jackson following the general's executions of two British citizens at St. Marks; in this image, Jackson defends himself. Perhaps the greatest American diplomat of his age, his acquisition of Florida has become legendary. (LC.)

Jackson is depicted in his private tent during the Creek Wars. He declined the governorship at least once and only accepted it with the condition that he would be permitted to resign as soon as the territorial government was organized. He departed west Florida in October, sending the president a resignation letter almost as an afterthought. Despite his limited governorship, he has been a dominant figure in Florida history. (AC.)

Jackson is seen here toward the end of his life at his home, the Hermitage. His mansion was the only place the old Indian fighter felt comfortable. By all accounts, he was not fond of Florida, and its modern appearance probably would have shocked him. In the 1950s, the Florida legislature voted to build a new executive mansion, with Old Hickory's beloved plantation for inspiration. (AC.)

Future president Zachary Taylor was a colonel in December 1837 when he led about 1,100 US troops on their way to Lake Okeechobee into an ambush that was a tactical victory for the 400 Seminoles, since Taylor had to retreat with much higher casualties than the natives. The Army declared it a strategic victory, promoted Taylor to brigadier general, and later, in May 1838, gave him overall command of Florida operations. (AC.)

In the election of 1876, the Republican nominee, Rutherford B. Hayes, lost the popular vote to Democrat Samuel Tilden, but the Electoral College vote was in doubt in Florida, Louisiana, Oregon, and South Carolina. A special election committee, after weeks of deliberation, awarded the election to Hayes. With Democrats openly threatening a second civil war, secret meetings were held between the national chairmen of both parties, and a deal was made. The Democrats would accept Hayes as president, and the Republicans would remove federal troops from the South. This one event would cause the collapse of Reconstruction and lead to 75 years of racial segregation and disenfranchisement. Overnight, Florida's Republican Party became obsolete, and the northern carpetbaggers, a major political force in state politics for a decade, quickly returned to the north. (AC.)

Seen here are images of American soldiers preparing to depart Florida. The 1st US Volunteer Cavalry Regiment, known as the "Rough Riders," were a diverse group, including Native Americans, Ivy League athletes, cowboys, gold prospectors, and former Texas rangers. Under Col. Theodore "Teddy" Roosevelt's command, they sailed to Cuba and fought in the historic battle on San Juan Hill. When the battleship USS *Maine* exploded in 1898, it propelled the United States into war with Spain. Perhaps no other state played more of a rule in the conflict than Florida. Invasion forces used Tampa as a base of operations, and several future governors fought valiantly in this much-romanticized conflict. (Both, LC.)

Teddy Roosevelt (far right) stands with other high-ranking officers of the Rough Riders in Tampa. By the end of 1898, the returning war hero was elected governor of New York and was selected to run for vice president in 1900 with William McKinley. Roosevelt became the 26th president in September 1901 following McKinley's assassination. (LC.)

Future president Teddy Roosevelt, always mindful of the press, poses for photographers by his tent during a brief strategy meeting with fellow Rough Riders. An avid outdoorsman, Roosevelt was a conservation-minded president. In 1903, he began the National Wildlife Refuge system by proclaiming Pelican Island near Vero Beach the first federal bird refuge. (Adam Baumel.)

A massive crowd in Jacksonville listens to President Roosevelt explain his desire for a Panama Canal. The concept of a canal in Central America was attractive for merchants on both coasts; for Floridians, it allowed for shorter sea travel to the Pacific. (LC.)

Florida governor David Sholtz was good friends with FDR and saw to it that Roosevelt's New Deal was promoted throughout the state; soon, nearly 50,000 Floridians were working in programs like the Civilian Conservation Corps (CCC). Young men from all over Florida would live in work camps and send the bulk of their paychecks home to their families. The CCC Museum at Highlands Hammock State Park honors the work done by these young men. (State Library and Archives of Florida.)

Pres. Harry Truman and Senator Pepper did not care for one another, and the feud led to Truman personally picking Florida congressman George Smathers to run against Pepper. What followed was one of the most controversial, expensive, and hateful elections in Florida History, which Smathers won in a walk. (Museum of Florida History.)

President Eisenhower's presidential airplane, the Constellation *Columbine II*, lands in Florida on his way to a summit. In 1948–1949, General Eisenhower held a series of meetings that resulted in the creation of the Department of Defense with President Truman in Key West. Eisenhower, like many other presidents, enjoyed the climate and ocean breezes of the Florida Keys. (LC.)

John F. Kennedy, during his brief tenure as the 35th president of the United States, left an impressive mark on the state of Florida—most notably, the three events presented here: consulting with his predecessor Dwight Eisenhower in Palm Beach following the Bay of Pigs, his involvement in establishing the space program, and the Cuban Missile Crisis. On October 22, 1961, at 7:00 p.m., Kennedy delivered a nationwide televised address announcing the discovery of the missiles. Florida was the center of national attention during the 13-day confrontation that pushed the world toward nuclear annihilation. (Both, AC.)

President Kennedy's 1961 goal of a manned lunar landing by 1970 required a dramatic expansion of existing space operations. Cape Canaveral was inadequate to host the new launch facility required for the mammoth 363-foot, 7.5 million–pound Saturn V rocket, which would be assembled vertically in a large hangar and transported on a mobile platform to one of several launch pads. Therefore, the decision was made to build a new Launch Operations site adjacent to Cape Canaveral on Merritt Island, the John F. Kennedy Space Center (left), part of Cape Canaveral Air Force Base. Many important events in the space race took place on this narrow strip of land. (Both, LC.)

Pres. Richard Nixon greets a jubilant crowd of supporters during a rally for the reelection campaign of Florida's Republican governor Claude Kirk, the first Republican to win the Florida governorship since Reconstruction. Throughout the 1968 campaign, Nixon developed a close friendship with the colorful Kirk, even being a surprise guest at the latter's 1967 wedding. Kirk lobbied hard throughout the 1968 primary season to be placed on the ticket as Nixon's vice president, forming a private political action committee and using a state airplane to travel across the country promoting his candidacy. Nixon did not select Kirk in 1968. Regardless, Nixon's popularity in the Sunshine State led to a convincing victory, as many Floridians saw the new president as a hometown boy. He campaigned hard for Kirk's unsuccessful 1970 reelection campaign, making trips to Tallahassee and Jacksonville. (AC.)

Ronald Reagan (center), in his first term as governor of California and a rising conservative star, speaks to supporters during a 1968 convention. Reagan lobbied hard for support from the Florida GOP during the 1968 primary season. He lost the nomination to former vice president Nixon, yet his convention speech helped catapult him onto the national stage. (LC.)

President Nixon greets supporters outside the 1972 Republican National Convention at the Miami Beach Convention Center. Despite the presence of demonstrators, the convention was a success, in sharp contrast to the disastrous Democratic convention held at the same venue. The incumbent Nixon overwhelmingly won Florida with 71.91 percent of the vote, carrying all 67 counties and 17 electoral votes. (LC.)

Pres. Gerald Ford is seen aboard Air Force One following a campaign rally in Florida. The 1976 campaign was a long and frustrating process for the president. He spent time and resources facing a serious challenge by Ronald Reagan for the nomination. Following the convention, he trailed the Democratic nominee Jimmy Carter by 20 points. (AC.)

President Ford shakes hands with a supporter dressed as Uncle Sam during a final swing across Florida, one of a handful of traditional bellwether states that the Ford campaign contested throughout the fall. As the polls became narrow, Ford spent more time in Florida. Ultimately, the strength of the state Democratic Party carried Carter to victory. (LC.)

Former Georgia governor and future Democratic nominee Jimmy Carter greets voters outside of a church in Jacksonville. During the 1976 primary election, the dark horse candidate focused on winning three early states: Iowa, New Hampshire, and Florida. As a result, he and his family spent most of the next 18 months in these states. Future first lady Rosalynn Carter was particularly determined to win the Florida primary and heavily lobbied its state legislature. In the 1976 election, the modern primary system was still in its infancy; as a result, Carter was the only candidate to compete in each of the 30 primaries across the country, a record amount at the time. Controversial Alabama governor George Wallace was the odds-on favorite to win the Florida primary, and all the other major Democratic candidates cleared the way for Carter to challenge him. After campaigning over 170 days in the Sunshine State, Carter narrowly won the primary election. (AC.)

Jimmy Carter works aboard "Peanut One," his 1976 campaign airplane, during a stop in Florida. Florida was deemed a likely Carter victory that November due in large part to his strength in the South. Regardless, he continued to make several stops across the state to secure its 17 electoral college votes. The state was called early for Carter, as he won by a margin of 5.29 percent. It would be the last time a Democratic presidential candidate won a majority of the north Florida counties, and as of the 2016 election, it was the last time Florida voted more Democratic than the national average. Both President and First Lady Carter actively campaigned for the state's Democratic Party for the next four years. As a sign of his popularity, many future candidates for statewide office adopted his campaign colors of green and white in their advertisements. (AC.)

Pres. George H.W. Bush, seen here with FEMA officials following Hurricane Andrew, had a decades-long relationship with south Florida. It began in 1943 when the young ensign trained at what was then Fort Lauderdale Naval Air Station—now Fort Lauderdale-Hollywood International Airport—and went on to become the Navy's youngest pilot. As vice president, Bush stopped nearby, holding a 1981 business roundtable at the iconic Lester's Diner on State Road 84. (LC.)

Vice President Bush visited Florida in 1988 following his election to the presidency, vacationing at the oceanfront town of Gulf Stream. He made many return trips while in the White House. When his son Jeb decided to enter the family business and run for office, the former president and his other son, Pres. George W. Bush, could be seen often throughout Jeb's governorship. (AC.)

Pres. George W. Bush is pictured at Booker Elementary School in Florida. The president was there for a photo op in a classroom when he received the news that the World Trade Center in New York had been struck by an airplane. "My reaction was, man, either the weather was bad or something extraordinary happened to the pilot," Bush later remembered. Once Bush received word that a second plane had crashed into the other tower, teachers in the room became anxious as the mood of the president turned grim. Bush waited several minutes before ending the event and addressing the nation. The next 10 years of American foreign policy began that day in central Florida. (Both, George W. Bush Presidential Library and Museum.)

Pres. Barack Obama waits backstage before delivering remarks at a reception for a Democratic Party fundraiser in Miami at the Fontainebleau Hotel. Obama brought out record numbers of voters during the 2008 general election and won the Sunshine State by three points. (LC.)

President Obama and Florida governor Charlie Crist talk while walking along the beach near the Pensacola Gulf Pier in Pensacola on June 15, 2010. This was the president's fourth trip to the Gulf Coast to assess the ongoing response to the BP oil spill in the Gulf of Mexico. (Photograph by Chuck Kennedy, courtesy of the White House.)

The Obamas embrace following a 2012 presidential debate in Florida. Earlier that year, the president gave a notable speech on the Magic Kingdom's Main Street, USA. President Obama noted that Disney theme parks "represent that quintessentially American spirit." Later that year, Obama visited Walt Disney World once again for the annual conference of the National Association of Latino Elected and Appointed Officials. (White House.)

President Obama watches the 2012 vice-presidential debate from the conference room of Air Force One on his way back from Florida. The president had made numerous trips to the Sunshine State throughout the year. He went on to barely win the state in his reelection. (Photograph by Chuck Kennedy, courtesy of the White House)

President Obama campaigns for Democratic nominee Hilary Clinton in the closing days of the 2016 election. Current presidents usually stay out of elections that determine who is going to replace them. However, Obama actively campaigned, and it was the first time since 2000 that a sitting two-term president campaigned in the Sunshine State. (LC.)

Pres. Donald Trump speaks inside the Vehicle Assembly Building following the launch of a SpaceX Falcon 9 rocket carrying the company's Crew Dragon spacecraft on NASA's SpaceX Demo-2 mission at the Kennedy Space Center. A new era of human spaceflight had begun, as American astronauts once again launched on an American rocket from American soil. (NASA/Bill Ingalls.)

Three

Fishing with the Presidents

This political cartoon is poking fun at the sportsman in chief, Teddy Roosevelt. The president was often featured in such images showcasing his energetic impulses to compete. Florida is the "Fishing Capital of the World," with more than three million anglers generating $9.6 billion in economic impact and supporting more than 128,000 jobs. To the surprise of no one, many American presidents have been anglers. (LC.)

Former president Theodore Roosevelt (left) and Russell J. Coles are pictured on a devilfish harpooning expedition on the coast of Florida in the winter of 1917. A true environmentalist as well as a sportsman, Roosevelt understood that wildlife must be preserved for future generations. During his second term, the National Forest Service and Roosevelt established Ocala National Forest in 1908. (LC.)

Pres. William Howard Taft travels aboard the ship *Phoenix* toward the end of his single term in office. The rivers, lakes, and saltwater around Stuart in Martin County have long been recognized for fabulous fishing. As a result, it has seen more than its share of presidential visits. In 1909, President Taft made the journey to Stuart and fished for sailfish to his heart's content. (LC.)

Future US president Gerald R. Ford Jr. (then known as Leslie Lynch King Jr.) holds a fishing rod and poses for a portrait in his home state of Michigan. It was not uncommon for young children to pose for such portraits at the time. (Gerald R. Ford Presidential Library.)

As the 29th US president, Warren G. Harding, seen above on his yacht, often vacationed in St. Augustine and Hollywood. Harding stayed at a hotel on Young Circle with a group of his friends. The image below shows the Hardings returning to the White House from Florida and being greeted by their dog Laddie Boy. Courtesy of John Ringling, Harding almost moved into a winter White House on Bird Key near Sarasota. Ringling had arranged for a mansion to be renovated with electric lighting, acetylene gas, and lavish furnishings. It took almost three years to complete the $100,000 project, but Harding never got to move in. He died suddenly of a heart attack in a San Francisco hotel. (Both, LC.)

From boyhood to adulthood, Herbert Hoover prized fishing as his favorite leisure activity. His friends, however, were amused that he often wore professional garb on his angling outings. His friend and National Park Service director Horace Albright commented in an interview that during his presidency, Hoover "fished in a blue-serge suit, double-breasted and with a high collar." (LC.)

President Hoover loved fishing in Florida and once held the record for the largest bonefish. His predecessor, Calvin Coolidge, also came frequently to Florida, spending a month once at the Mount Dora Inn and visiting relatives in Orlando. He also played a role in a fraudulent doctored image involving Coolidge by a giant tree that was a major tourist attraction in Longwood before it burned down. (LC.)

Hoover was a prolific writer upon leaving the White House, addressing the topic of fishing in the article "Men are Equal before the Fish," for a Florida magazine in 1951 and later publishing a memoir, *Fishing for Fun: And to Wash Your Soul*, about his relationship with the sport: "Fishing is a chance to wash one's soul with pure air, with the rush of the brook, or with the shimmer of the sun on the blue water." (LC.)

Franklin Roosevelt is pictured with the 500-pound, seven-foot-long jewfish his son Elliot caught on March 21, 1926, at Jewfish Creek. From 1924 to 1926, believing that warm water and air would help him walk again, he spent winters on his new houseboat, the 71-foot *Larooco*, sailing the Florida Keys, fishing, swimming, playing parcheesi, entertaining guests, and tending to engine mishaps. (LC.)

FDR relaxes on a sunny Florida beach with friends Missy, Maunselle S. Crosby, and Frances F.de Rham. The future president's weak and disabled legs are clearly visible. From having his car converted so it could appear that he was driving to hiding his legs in the ocean, Roosevelt went to great lengths to hide his disability. (LC.)

Franklin Roosevelt, Maunselle Crosby, and Oswald Mosley pose in the Florida water. Despite attempts to project physical strength, it is obvious that the New York governor is merely sitting in the water and not swimming. It was always important for Roosevelt to be presented alongside youthful and strong associates. (LC.)

Numerous presidents have enjoyed the sport of fishing. From Washington to Trump, it is the favorite pastime of all presidents. FDR, seen here, was an avid, lifelong fisherman. With his lack of mobility after contracting polio, he used fishing as a discreet way to relax away from the press. Ever the politician, he also used the sport to further his agendas. During World War II, President Roosevelt fished with British prime minister Winston Churchill at Shangri-La (now Camp David) in Maryland's Catoctin Mountains, where they planned the invasion of Sicily. (Both, LC.)

President Roosevelt greets fans during a trip to south Florida. While his homestead in New York was where he was most comfortable, he had been coming to the Florida Keys after his defeat in the 1920 presidential election. The sea-loving Roosevelt purchase a large boat and spent many years relaxing aboard it. (LC.)

For Roosevelt's health, his wife, Eleanor, felt compelled to visit the boat, but she disliked the atmosphere: "I tried fishing but had no skill and no luck; when we anchored at night and the wind blew, it all seemed eerie and menacing to me." (Franklin D. Roosevelt Presidential Library and Museum.)

Sometimes, Roosevelt went to the dunes in an old bathing suit, found a secluded spot, and crawled on his hands and knees over the hot sand until he was worn out. Back at his rented cottage, he would fix drinks for himself and friends. He did not mind crawling because he could do that himself; what he hated was for others to have to carry him from place to place. (LC.)

President Truman may have enjoyed freshwater fishing in his beloved Missouri, but when it came to saltwater fishing in the Keys, he would have much preferred to sightsee or read. Ever accommodating, the president felt he owed it to his Florida boosters and fans to take part in their fishing trips. It was First Lady Bess Truman who really enjoyed the sport; by all accounts, she excelled at it. (LC.)

David Eisenhower, the grandson of President Eisenhower, fishes with his wife, Julie Nixon Eisenhower, in Key Biscayne in 1971. Due to his connections with Presidents Nixon and Eisenhower, David was one of the inspirations for the 1969 Creedence Clearwater Revival song "Fortunate Son," and is the namesake of Camp David, the famous presidential retreat. (LC.)

Future president Gerald Ford is seen deep-sea fishing with his wife, Betty. The Fords took numerous vacations throughout the year and had a personal love for Florida. President Ford, in particular, loved the state's many golf courses and played with actor Jackie Gleason at the Lago Mar Country Club in Fort Lauderdale. (LC.)

There is no documentation about Ford catching any fish during this vacation in 1966; however, he did catch up on some sleep. As president, Ford still found time to relax. He was a natural athlete and enjoyed all kinds of sports, especially golf (18 handicap while president), swimming, tennis, horseback riding, and taking the family on skiing trips to Vail, Colorado. Ford often said he was not interested in fishing and that he was always more into team sports, which is ironic considering that he spent most of his retirement playing golf and swimming in his pool. Despite this supposed indifference, Ford signed into law the landmark fishery legislation that is now known as the Magnuson-Stevens Fishery Conservation and Management Act, which has helped to preserve the nation's rich fishing grounds for generations. (Gerald R. Ford Presidential Library.)

President Carter is putting on his wading boots for a day of fishing. In his book *Sharing Good Times*, the president mentions his love for fishing and shares stories about exploits across the globe, catching fish on each continent. The first occupant of the White House to reach 96 years of age, Carter still regularly fishes. (LC.)

President and First Lady Carter fish while on vacation during the summer of 1979. Recently, the former president spent the holidays vacationing in the Florida Keys with Rosalynn and other family members. During one holiday season, Carter was part of a group that went on a fishing trip out of Hawk's Cay Resort & Marina in Marathon, led by noted captain Rich Tudor. The group caught more than 70 fish and took home about 15 snapper and Spanish mackerel. (LC.)

In the 1970s, George H.W. Bush often visited the Cheeca Lodge on Islamorada in the Florida Keys to go bonefishing. A frequent freshwater fisherman, he is seen here focusing on the clear waters of the Keys while traveling during his vice presidency. After serving as the 41st president, he co-founded the George Bush Cheeca Lodge Bonefish Tournament in 1994, which raised money for various charities. (LC.)

Four

A Thousand Rounds of Golf

President Taft is seen aboard a train in south Florida. The trip's leisurely pace afforded him time to hit the golf course, his favorite sport. Florida is known for its golf courses, and each president who has stopped in Florida has usually found time to visit the state's beautiful courses. Their games varied as widely as their presidencies, yet it has always provided the busy commander in chief with a welcome break from the business of the presidency. (LC.)

"For God's sake, don't let the reporters see you golf," was the advice President Roosevelt had for his successor during the 1908 presidential election. In many people's minds, golf was considered a sport of the wealthy, and contrasted with the images many politicians had cultivated as humble citizens serving the public. But Taft did not mind and always allowed members of the press to see him play. (LC.)

Pres. Warren Harding, an avid golfer, is seen here taking advantage of the state's warm climate. First Lady Florence Harding suffered from severe kidney disease for much of her adult life. The ocean breezes and sunshine of Florida were a welcome respite from her frequent pain. The president traveled with his wife during the congressional summer recess and would often have to be dragged from the golf course. (LC.)

On many weekends, the current president of the United States plays golf in Florida. Almost a century ago, another US president, Warren G. Harding, also golfed in Florida. And when he did, most of that time, he was playing on a St. Augustine course. With his new position, reporters followed him everywhere, including the golf course. Harding requested that the reporters respect his privacy while he golfed. He admitted that he played a lot of golf but never improved. He promised the reporters that he would tell them of anything newsworthy that took place while he played. He told them it would be real news if he broke 100. Sometimes, professional golfer Jim Barnes was his partner. Barnes won the US Open in 1921 and the British Open in 1925. (LC.)

There was a joke that the choice for postmaster general would be decided by a game of golf. But Harding declined the challenge, saying that he was "unwilling to have the administration weakened by basing its aptitude on my incapacity of golf." Harding would return to St. Augustine to play golf in 1922 and 1923. It was, without question, his favorite golfing destination in the Sunshine State. (LC.)

One day in 1922, Harding got in 36 holes of golf—18 before lunch and 18 in the afternoon. Harding played at other courses up and down the east coast of Florida. After a week of less-than-stellar golf, he headed south by yacht, with stops in Rockledge, Brevard County, and eventually Vero Beach, playing golf along the way. (LC.)

President Eisenhower takes a break after a heated game in Florida. Without question, Eisenhower was the finest of the presidential putters. Despite having a bad swing, his love of the sport should earn him a place in the World Golf Hall of Fame. While none of the presidents have been described as serious players of the game, Eisenhower is the only one to make a hole in one. As the golfer in chief, Eisenhower brought golf to the White House lawn and played nearly 800 rounds while in office. He was a constant presence at the Masters and seemed to fit his schedule around the day's tee time. He played so much golf in the White House that the oval office floor had to be replaced due to his golf shoes. (LC.)

President Nixon and his wife, Pat, with Tricia Nixon, are on a golf cart in front of Marine One at their home in Key Biscayne. Despite living near many world-renowned golf courses in south Florida, the 37th president was not the most active of golfers. His favorite pastimes were bowling and reading. (Museum of Florida History.)

President Ford was a great athlete; he played on two national championship football teams at Michigan. He was also an accomplished swimmer, doing daily laps into his 90s. He was, however, a pretty poor golfer, yet he adored the sport. (LC.)

This is a photograph of President Reagan putting a golf ball around Air Force One with members of his cabinet looking on. Reagan did not play much but was said to have a powerful swing. His most significant golf moment came when playing a round at Augusta Country Club while an armed man crashed the gates, took hostages, and demanded to talk to Reagan. (LC.)

President Obama is seen in central Florida during the closing days of the 2012 election. Florida is one of the most important battleground states in the nation, causing Obama to make multiple trips to the state. Of course, like every president, Obama made good use of the numerous recreational options. While playing at the Floridian National Gold Golf Course, he hit the links with Tiger Woods in a much-publicized match. Throughout his two terms, Obama was often seen on the golf course. His frequent rounds were often criticized by commentators and the opposing party. Obama averaged 42 rounds of golf a year, while the current president averages 87, but neither come close to Woodrow Wilson or Dwight Eisenhower, who are estimated to have played 150 and 100 rounds per year, respectively. (White House.)

President Trump is seen at the Trump International Golf Club. Donald Trump has been closely associated with the sport of golf for decades. Perhaps no other American president has played as much golf in Florida. It helps that he owns several resorts with their own golf courses. He even has his own golf organization, Trump Golf, founded in 1999 with the mission to create the world's best luxury golf experience that celebrates the purity of the game, family values, and tradition. With 16 courses from Dubai to the West Coast, the president has played many of them during his time in the White House. (White House.)

Five

The Little White House

The presidential plane touches down in Florida. In November 1946, Pres. Harry S. Truman had finished 19 months in office but was physically exhausted. His doctor, Wallace Graham, ordered a warm vacation. Truman selected a charming two-story house within the naval station at Key West. As he was leaving, he promised to return whenever he felt the need for rest. Truman used the Little White House 11 times, spending 175 days of his presidency there. (LC.)

President Truman's Douglas VC-118, the *Independence*, was named in honor of his hometown of Independence, Missouri. This presidential plane, with its unique, bright color scheme, and dramatic front stylized to look like an eagle, was an exciting arrival. Floridians had become used to seeing their presidents, but official presidential planes were a different matter. Air travel was still a novelty in 1946, and this was a sight some old-timers still talk about. (LC.)

A refreshed Harry Truman returns to Washington, DC, from his prolonged vacation in Key West. Notice the large official party exiting the plane behind him. As Truman grew more comfortable in the office of president, he started to stretch out the length of his trips to Key West. As Nancy Reagan would later famously remark, the office comes with the president—not that aides much cared. The change of climate was greatly appreciated by all. (LC.)

First Daughter Margaret Truman, seen here in the presidential limousine, often traveled with her parents to Key West. "We needed a rest almost as much as he did," she recalled. Shortly after she and her mother arrived for one vacation, reporters and other members of Truman's Key West tribe mounted a mock victory parade, wearing what Margaret Truman called "the wackiest costumes you have ever seen in your life." (LC.)

Bess and Margaret Truman wait at the airport for the return of President Truman from Florida. The two women in the president's life had joined him earlier on his Key West vacation, yet they always returned home long before him. Aides always noted that he was more restless when away from his girls—except when his wife and daughter visited, it was a masculine world. (LC.)

A delighted Harry Truman waves his hat to a crowd of Key West well-wishers as he enters the former naval station (later named Truman Annex) in Key West. Truman is a rarity among presidential vacationers to the Sunshine State. He seems to be the only president who made his first visit to the state while in office and made it his official vacation residence. (LC.)

The annex got its start in 1845 as part of Fort Zachary Taylor, a US Army installation. The base was eventually taken over in 1947 as the Fort Zachary Taylor Annex to Naval Station Key West. New docks had been added in 1932 to make it a base for submarines. The station was mostly decommissioned in 1974 because contemporary nuclear submarines were too large to use it. (LC.)

Other presidents to use the house have included William Howard Taft in 1912, Dwight Eisenhower in 1955–1956, and John Kennedy in 1961 and 1962. Former presidents Jimmy Carter in 1996 and 2007 and Bill Clinton in 2005 also used the house over the years. President Kennedy and British prime minister Harold Macmillan held a one-day summit here in March 1961. (LC.)

President Truman is pictured in an informal shirt alongside friend and White House press secretary Joseph Short. Around this time in 1948, Truman met with the Joint Chiefs of Staff to hammer out the creation of the Department of Defense. This was called the Key West Agreement. (LC.)

Seen here are images of President Truman (seated on couch at center above and at right below) with his staff and members of the press, most decked out in beachwear. Friends remembered that a Key West vacation was a succession of happy days. "I doubt I've ever been as tired in my life," aide Clark Clifford said. "I remember I went . . . without shaving, just as part of the general celebration following the 1948 election. And we loafed; we didn't discuss any serious business. I don't know how the government ran during that time; we were utterly exhausted! I remember going down for a while, sleeping about 14 hours a day, and then lolling around on the beach." (Both, LC.)

The presidential party gets ready to board the yacht *Williamsburg.* Truman liked the easy banter at Truman Beach—or in a fishing boat or at the poker table, which might be called the true center of a Truman vacation. Truman would tell his aide Rigdon, "Bill, round up a quorum." Soon, the president and other men were pulling up chairs around the poker table made for him by sailors at the submarine base. Many thought he loved the games mostly for the ribbing that punctuated play. "Getting together with his old friends with whom he was completely comfortable was the greatest relaxation he had," aide Clark Clifford remembered. Truman bet freely and often, liked wild cards, oddball variations of the game, and an occasional bluff. Fellow players said he enjoyed himself even while holding losing hands. (LC.)

President Truman chats with members of his official party following another fishing trip. The coral island of Key West—four miles long and two miles wide—is the southernmost point in the continental United States. It is also an excellent place for saltwater fishing. Aboard the presidential yacht *Williamsburg*, the party would deep-sea fish for yellowfin, grouper, amberjack, mackerel, and even barracuda. (LC.)

President Truman works at his desk inside the Little White House. National legislation was drafted and official government business was conducted daily from this site. Perhaps the most important of these actions occurred on December 5, 1951, when Truman enacted a civil rights executive order requiring federal contractors to hire minorities. (LC.)

The president quickly settled into a Key West routine. He rose as early as 7:00 a.m. and took a bracing morning walk, ranging the tree-shaded streets of the base and sometimes venturing into town. The *Williamsburg* docked nearby to offer communications and logistical support. Its crew had breakfast ready when Truman returned to the Little White House, usually around 8:00 a.m. The president was often joined at the breakfast table by members of his senior staff, some of whom shared the house with him. They might have included Fleet Adm. William Leahy, his chief of staff; William D. Hassett, his correspondence secretary; or Clark Clifford, chief counsel, speechwriter, and political tactician. (Both, LC.)

The president's personal physician, Gen. Wallace Graham, poses with his catch of the day. Besides Bess and Margaret, the entire presidential entourage were middle-aged men who held a variety of civil service posts. From members of the military's top brass, high-ranking cabinet members, mid-ranking office aides, and military advisors, it made no difference. There was only one president and one boss, and everyone else was treated as equals. It was a glorious time: the country was at peace, the economy was entering its postwar boom, and Harry S. Truman was turning into a beach bum. (LC.)

President Truman (in white hat) is on the afterdeck of the *Williamsburg* during a vacation in Key West with, among others, Charles Murphy, special counsel to the president (far left); Adm. Robert Dennison, naval aide to the president (second from right, in uniform); and Charles Ross, press secretary (far right). When not on the boat, Truman would following breakfast work on his mail until about 10:00 a.m., then gathered aides and walked with them to Truman Beach to soak up the sun. When Truman was ready, he took off his sun helmet and went in for a swim. A lover of cold water, the secret service agents had to stay in the water if he did, often making them shiver in the cold, salty surf. After lunch, it was a nap, followed by a marathon poker game, and then the big production of dinner. (LC.)

These images are from one of the many fishing excursions President Truman took during his time in Florida. Truman was never an eager fisherman. "He is a man who can take his fishing or leave it alone," *Time* magazine said. During one trip, the president boarded the Navy crash boat *Dolphin* for three hours of deep-sea fishing. At day's end, photographers recorded his catch: a Spanish mackerel, a five-pound barracuda, and a grouper. There would be more fishing. But for the president, the clear highlight of this particular vacation came after Sunday dinner on March 16, when the staff joined him to listen to Margaret Truman's professional singing debut in a radio concert broadcast from Detroit. The proud father was overwhelmed by the first daughter's performance. (Both, LC.)

President Truman takes in the sea air with aides above and signs the registry for Fort Jefferson below. Vacations in Key West were a time for relaxation and for Truman to indulge in his passions, with more time for reading, thinking, and socializing. Truman often displayed his love of history at Key West. Aide Joseph G. Feeney said that one night the talk at the Little White House turned to famous military conflicts. Truman arranged four sets of silverware on a table, and he and press secretary Charlie Ross fought out 14 major battles in world history, moving the knives, forks, and spoons to represent armies and divisions. (Both, LC.)

Above, President Truman and his party relax in the shady courtyard of Fort Jefferson (seen from the air below) after a full day of sightseeing. Truman loved to take his party to historic locations like this and enjoyed his reputation as Key West's number-one vacationer. It took him two years of searching to find this picture-perfect locale. Despite his best efforts, he never warmed up to Shangri-La (later renamed Camp David), the heavily wooded camp Franklin D. Roosevelt had enjoyed in the mountains of western Maryland. A search began for a warm-weather place that could accommodate not only the president, but 15 staff members, 15 or so Secret Service agents, and 20 to 30 reporters and photographers. Key West checked all the boxes and provided the working-class president with six years' worth of all-inclusive resort living. (Both, LC.)

This is a view of the Little White House during one of Truman's trips to Key West. The sun, palm trees, beach, and easy atmosphere made all the president's vacations memorable and relaxing. "The sun shines with terrific force down here," Truman reported to Bess. "My face and head are as red as a beet, but the rest of me is brown." (LC.)

President Truman speaks to the graduating 1949 naval sonar class at Key West Naval Station. After Truman won his election in 1948, the Navy had the house professionally redecorated, hanging maritime paintings and prints borrowed from the US Naval Academy. Impressed with the new style and comfort of the place, Truman told Bess, "I've a notion to move the Capitol to Key West and just stay." (LC.)

President Truman (far right) is pictured with Pres. Rómulo Gallegos of Venezuela (far left). Truman insisted, as many presidents have, that much work went with him to Key West, reminding the public that presidential holidays were more of a change of scenery than true vacations. Truman, by his estimation, signed his name 600 times a day on bills, proclamations, executive orders, and letters. At a shirt-sleeves news conference on the lawn of the Little White House following a goodwill cruise aboard the *Williamsburg* in the Caribbean, Truman insisted he was not wasting time on vacation: "I have been in touch with the State Department every day since we have been away." By then, the publicity given Truman's Key West vacations had created a tourist boom. New air-conditioned resorts and motels appeared, adding new luster to a somewhat shabby town whose rows of cheap bars catered mostly to off-duty sailors. "New stores are opening, restaurants are crowded, the sidewalks are flowing with women in shorts and halters, and men in atom-flash sports shirts," *Time* magazine reported. (LC.)

President Truman (right) is in an open Lincoln Cosmopolitan limousine with Pres. Miguel Alemán Valdés of Mexico. By the time of Truman's fourth trip to Key West in February 1947, speculation was building on whether he would run for election in his own right in 1948. Most pundits told him not to bother. *Time* said the Democrats "seemed to be heading for the ditch," with voters apparently ready to "dump the whole Truman administration." But *Time's* reporter was surprised to find no evidence of concern on Truman Beach. The president was tanned, carefree, and smiling, he reported. Chief counsel Clark Clifford "glistened with confidence and sunburn oil." The election of 1948 ended with Truman winning his historic upset victory, soon followed with him boarding the *Independence* and flying to Florida for a rest. "Key West never before had seen such a celebration," reported the *Miami Herald*. The Associated Press stated that people stood 10 to 20 feet deep along the sidewalks. (LC.)

Pres. John F. Kennedy is pictured at Key West Naval Station in November 1962. JFK was a great admirer of Harry Truman, famously asking for the former president's autograph during his post-inaugural luncheon in 1961. Here, the 35th president begins what would be a long day trip across Key West, including a stop at Key West High School. (LC.)

President Kennedy (right), with British prime minister Harold Macmillan, held a one-day summit at the Little White House in March 1961. Kennedy made a second visit in 1962 immediately following the Cuban Missile Crisis. Many presidents have come to Truman's Little White House over the years, feeling a connection to their praised predecessor. (LC.)

Six

WINTER WHITE HOUSE

From Camelot to Mar-a-Lago, Palm Beach is loaded with presidential sites. President Kennedy, seen here departing a US Navy ship during a trip to Key West, can be felt across this part of Florida, from the Kennedy family compound where the president and his family came to recharge to a secret fallout shelter designed to save the president from nuclear attack. (LC.)

During the 1920s, south Florida enjoyed great prosperity. It was the height of the state's land boom, and a massive influx of money was pouring in. The entire state was rapidly becoming one of the most popular leisure and travel destinations in the country, but with the stock market crash in 1929 and the Great Depression that followed, the state's economy crashed overnight. The land boom left behind entire new cities, such as Coral Gables, Hialeah, Miami Springs, Opa-Locka, Miami Shores, and Hollywood. However, the bust left behind numerous failed development projects. What was once the playground of old and wealthy families was now accessible to social climbers. Kennedy took advantage of the sagging property markets. (Both, LC.)

Senator and Jacqueline Kennedy are pictured here with their wedding party, which included future US senator George Smathers. A day or two after the 1960 presidential election, John Fitzgerald Kennedy came to Palm Beach with his valet and secretary, his wife, a nurse for the children, a maid, and a private secretary. An adjacent beach house was filled with cooks, maids, pool men, chauffeurs, and hairdressers. There was also a retinue of Secret Service agents and reporters. One reporter later described the scene as a "screwball comedy." The Kennedy presidency had strong ties to Palm Beach. JFK was particularly fond of the burgers at nearby Hamburger Heaven and went to Sunday Mass at Saint Edward's Church, where his favorite pew near the back of the church is marked with a "JFK worshipped here" plaque. (Both, LC.)

The Kennedy's Palm Beach estate was designed in 1923 for Rodman Wanamaker of Philadelphia by noted society architect Addison Mizner. With its simplified Mediterranean-style architecture, the house was originally named "La Querida," which loosely translates as "the dear one." Boston-based Joseph P. Kennedy Sr., the Kennedy patriarch, bought the house in 1933 as a winter retreat for his family, including his wife, Rose, and their children. After giving birth to her son in 1960, Jacqueline Kennedy recuperated here. After it became the Winter White House, Kennedy would spend time playing golf at the Palm Beach Country Club and go sailing. In November 1963, the president spent the weekend in Palm Beach before his assassination in Dallas. (LC.)

This station is closely associated with Pres. John F. Kennedy and the tensions of the Cuban Missile Crisis in 1961 and 1962. The government acquired the land in 1961, and a fallout shelter was built in secrecy. Its purpose was to serve as a command center for the president should there have been a nuclear attack while he was visiting his family's nearby Palm Beach home. The station, a two-story frame Colonial Revival–style structure built in 1936, served as a base for coastal patrols and rescue missions during World War II. There is also a boathouse. The docks were destroyed by Hurricane Irma in September 2017. The bulk of 80-acre Peanut Island, just inside the Lake Worth Inlet, also known as the Palm Beach Inlet, is a county park. Today, it is a popular weekend spot for boaters, swimmers, fishermen, and snorkelers and offers campsites, picnic tables, and a hiking trail. (LC.)

President Kennedy addressed the nation from the Oval Office during the impending Cuban quarantine. In response to the failed Bay of Pigs invasion of 1961 and the presence of American Jupiter ballistic missiles in Italy and Turkey, Soviet leader Nikita Khrushchev agreed to Cuba's request to place nuclear missiles on the island to deter a future invasion. What followed was several days of intense negotiations between the two countries. President Kennedy and Secretary of Defense McNamara supported a naval blockade of Cuba. According to international law, a blockade was an act of war. Yet the Kennedy administration felt that it was a more peaceful method of dealing with the presence of nuclear missiles in Cuba than the other option of an airstrike against the missile bases. Ultimately, the blockade worked, and the missiles were removed. (LC.)

President Nixon's compound in Key Biscayne is pictured here at sunset. Nixon purchased the first of his three waterfront homes, 500 Bay Lane, in 1969 from his former Senate colleague George Smathers of Florida. Nixon visited it at least 50 times while in office from 1969 to 1974. A native Californian, Nixon preferred to retreat to south Florida because he loved the warmth and ambiance. He enjoyed dining at Joe's Stone Crabs and drinking at local taverns. He also loved the ocean breeze and was always happy on the water, where he could find privacy. (LC.)

In 1968, Miami Beach landed the Republican National Convention, in no small part because the nominee, Richard Nixon, had a house on Key Biscayne close to his friend Bebe Rebozo, founder of the Key Biscayne Bank. Miami Beach, which is a separate city from Miami and is on an island off the coast, had a key advantage over other locations. Access to the island was possible only over three bridges, which the police could easily block to keep demonstrators away. However, at the height of the Watergate scandal, protesters still found a way onto the property. More than one protester took a nap on the president's helipad. According to administration officials, during the crisis, Key Biscayne was the only place outside of the White House where the president felt comfortable. (LC.)

Before winning the 1968 election, Nixon purchased a three-bedroom home on Key Biscayne and visited it frequently while in office. Some in the media suspected that Nixon's good friend Bebe Rebozo, a known mob associate, facilitated that purchase. Nixon was also criticized after $400,000 in federal funds were used to build a helicopter pad near the one-story Winter White House. (LC.)

Though occasionally visited by military and foreign advisers, Nixon preferred not to conduct presidential business in Key Biscayne. Yet while there, historians believe he and his high-level advisers concocted the scheme to break into the Democratic National Committee headquarters at the Watergate Hotel in Washington. (LC.)

When Nixon sold his property, including the helicopter pad, there were public accusations that he enriched himself at taxpayer expense. Later, the 1983 gangster movie *Scarface*, starring Al Pacino, was filmed on the property. Not long after, the historic property was destroyed by developers—a common fate in the Sunshine State. (LC.)

President and Pat Nixon walk along the beach. Even in these candid moments, the president still carried an aura of formality. During the summer, Secret Service agents would find Nixon camped out by the pool, reading a newspaper, and wearing a suit. Regardless, in recent years, the Key Biscayne Sandbar, located near Nixon's old Winter White House, has become known as the Nixon Sandbar, with very different attire options. (LC.)

The 1972 Republican National Convention was scheduled for San Diego, but Nixon decided to go back to Miami Beach, near his winter home. He did not care that the Democrats were also holding their convention in Miami Beach that year. It would be the last time both parties' national conventions were in the same city. (LC.)

The contrasting quality of the Nixon White House is perfectly encapsulated by this one image at the Winter White House of the president with his best friend and associate Bebe Rebozo alongside the leadership of the FBI. Rebozo (far left), president and owner of the Key Biscayne Bank, was indicted for money laundering a $100,000 donation from Howard Hughes to the Nixon election campaign. (LC.)

The legacy of the Key Biscayne Winter White House lives on today in Plains, Georgia, of all places. The Carter Compound, shown here, in the heart of the Jimmy Carter National Historic Site in Plains, was purchased by the government as a future addition to the historic site. The Carters were granted lifetime residence. The home is maintained by the National Park Service, and the former first family is protected by the Secret Service. Originally, a simple gatehouse and barrier were placed at both entrances of the compound during the 1976 election. This is a common practice until a candidate is elected and more permanent protection is needed. After the sale of Nixon's home in Key Biscayne, its massive gate was shipped to Plains. (LC.)

Seven

Mar-a-Lago

Pres. Donald Trump likes to call Mar-a-Lago—his Palm Beach club and catering facility—the "Winter White House," and while that is just his nickname for the estate, there is some speculation that it will become official after the president changed his residency from New York to Florida. For many Floridians, this transfer gave the state a status it always lacked: a presidential home state. (LC.)

Mar-a-Lago is a resort and national historic landmark built from 1924 to 1927 by cereal-company heiress and socialite Marjorie Merriweather Post. The 126-room, 62,500-square-foot mansion is in Palm Beach County on the Palm Beach barrier island, with the Atlantic Ocean to the east and Florida's Intracoastal Waterway to the west. The structure is a far cry from the "simple cabin by the sea" that its original owner professed to want. Post paid for the house to be built as a second residence for her and then-husband Edward F. Hutton. She hired Marion Sims Wyeth to design it and Joseph Urban to create interior design and exterior decorations. Post spent $7 million, equivalent to $103 million in 2020. (LC.)

Marine One lands at the resort during the Thanksgiving holiday season in 2017. Throughout his first year in office, President Trump used this resort as the site of many family gatherings and public events. He has stated that he feels more comfortable here than in the White House, which was under renovation during much of his first year in office. (LC.)

This is a postcard of Palm Beach during the time of the mansion's construction. Architects Marion Sims Wyeth and Joseph Urban designed the estate, which sits on 20 acres. Wyeth also designed the Florida governor's mansion in Tallahassee. (LC.)

Here is a view of the kitchen wing of the mansion in the 1970s. The club has an exclusive membership of 500 paying members and admits 20 to 40 new members a year. Members include oil executive Bill Koch, financier Thomas Peterffy, New Jersey Democratic Party leader George Norcross, lobbyist Kenneth Duberstein, and real estate developers Bruce E. Toll and Richard LeFrak. (LC.)

This is a view from the top of the resort's tower. As part of his renovation of the property, Trump commandeered a coat of arms that British authorities granted in 1939 to Joseph Edward Davies, Post's third husband, replacing "*Integritas*," the Latin word for integrity, with "Trump." He also spent $100,000 on four gold-plated sinks. (LC.)

Post, who died in 1973, willed the 17-acre estate to the US government for use by presidents and visiting foreign dignitaries. Mar-a-Lago was declared a national historic landmark in 1980. In 1981, the government returned Mar-a-Lago to the Post Foundation, citing its high annual maintenance cost of $1 million. Happily, while surrounding homes were being demolished to make way for smaller modern homes, Mar-a-Lago remained untouched. This is when the future president stepped in. Trump's reported first offer for the property—$28 million—was turned down. But he persisted, and the market slumped. Trump ended up getting the property for $5 million in 1985 and paid an additional $3 million for Post's antiques and furniture. Trump turned Mar-a-Lago into a private club in 1995 and built a 20,000-square-foot ballroom with $7 million in gold leaf. The vast structure has received praise from some locals and has maintained its reputation as one of the most celebrated homes in Florida. (LC.)

Donald Trump has not always had a pleasant relationship with his adopted home town of Palm Beach. In 2006, he installed an 80-foot pole, despite Palm Beach ordinances forbiding flag poles higher than 42 feet; a violation carries a daily fine of $250. Trump sued for $25 million, claiming his right to free speech was being violated. Ultimately, he and the town came to an agreement: Trump switched to a smaller flag on a 70-foot pole. And instead of paying fines, he donated $100,000 to veterans' charities. In 2016, Trump sued Palm Beach County for what he called "deliberate and malicious" actions for moving flight paths from Palm Beach International Airport over Mar-a-Lago. It is now a moot point as the Secret Service requested a no-fly zone be established over Mar-a-Lago when Trump is in residence. (LC.)

Here is a view from the second story looking out over the sea. The house has 58 bedrooms, 33 bathrooms, a 29-foot-long pietra dura marble-top dining table, 12 fireplaces, and three bomb shelters. (LC.)

The entrance hall is pictured here looking toward the main entrance. The property is covered in Spanish tiles, Italian marble, and Venetian silks. When Donald Trump purchased the property, his wife at the time, Ivana, was charged with running it. Trump retained Mar-a-Lago through both his divorces. His family maintains private quarters in a separate, closed-off area of the house and grounds. (LC.)

The resort's main library is a private presidential study that would have made bookworms John Adams and Thomas Jefferson jealous. The massive room is paneled with centuries-old British oak and filled with rare first-edition books. There are reportedly a few signed copies of *The Art of the Deal* there as well. (LC.)

Seen here is the main entrance of the property during its transition from a private home to an exclusive resort. In early 2017, following Trump's November 2016 election victory, the initiation fee for new members was reportedly increased to $200,000. According to records, Mar-a-Lago is one of Trump's most profitable businesses. He made $15.6 million from the club in 2014. (LC.)

The resort's entrance gate, seen here in 2014, serves as one of its most imposing aspects. It is also a bridge between the more muted tastes of the Post family and the flashier tastes of Trump. The glamorous Post rooms were given a layer of gold leaf. (LC.)

The first family departs for the resort on Marine One in 2017. In November 2017, President Trump returned to Mar-a-Lago for his first presidential Thanksgiving celebration, and one month later, he returned for his 10th presidential visit during his Christmas vacation. He addressed members of the US armed services during both holidays from his private office. (LC.)

When he opened Mar-a-Lago, Trump welcomed Jewish members and African Americans, who had been prohibited from joining other Palm Beach clubs. Club members reportedly used to pay a $100,000 initiation fee and annual dues of $14,000 (along with taxes and an annual food minimum of $2,000) for the privilege of using the facilities. (LC.)

Workers prepare for an official event at Mar-a-Lago. President Trump has used his resort as an effective home-court advantage during his negotiations with national and world leaders. In what the resort calls "Trump Season," a large cluster of events are held weekly, with everything from fundraisers, balls, and state dinners. (LC.)

President Trump boards Air Force One following a trip to Mar-a-Lago. Trump has referred to Mar-a-Lago as his winter White House and moved his official residency from New York to Florida in 2019, making him the first Floridian president in history. (LC.)

An animatronic statue of President Trump speaks to the audience during Disney's Hall of Presidents ride. The past four US presidents have all provided recordings for the ever-changing presentation. Housed in a building resembling Philadelphia's Independence Hall, the attraction currently features a short film depicting a historical account of several American presidencies, notably George Washington, Andrew Jackson, Abraham Lincoln, Theodore Roosevelt, Franklin D. Roosevelt, and John F. Kennedy. (LC.)

President Trump meets with Pres. Michel Temer of Brazil at Mar-a-Lago. During the Trump administration, the Sunshine State seems to have finally received its wish: the right to call itself a presidential home state. With this distinction comes the possibility that Florida may also one day be the site of a presidential library and museum. This prospect has already been rumored, with many communities longing to house the Donald J. Trump library. The old town of Briny Breezes occupies 43 acres of prime waterfront land between the Atlantic and the Intracoastal Waterway, just 12 miles south of Mar-a-Lago, and has been seen as a likely site. (State Library and Archives of Florida.)

Eight

The Allure of the Sunshine State

Theodore Roosevelt was one of the most fascinating people in the nation's history. The youngest and most vigorous president at the time, he was also a champion of conservation. His impressive contributions nationwide can sometimes outshine his efforts to preserve wildlife in Florida. Thanks to Roosevelt, Floridians have been able to maintain hundreds of thousands of acreage of natural wilderness. Historian Douglas Brinkley proclaimed him "the president who saved Florida." (LC.)

The Presidents Hall of Fame is one of Florida's oldest remaining roadside attractions. Located in Clermont, it is also home to a White House replica and presidential wax museum. Once described by Ronald Reagan as a "true national treasure," it contains one of the largest collections of presidential memorabilia in the world. The White House replica is the crown jewel of the collection. Its detailed and elaborate interiors are so acclaimed that it was once placed on display in the actual executive mansion. Other highlights are replicas of the Lincoln Memorial, Mount Rushmore, and oval office. A portion of the mansion's famed East Room is also displayed, as is a former presidential limousine. (Both, LC.)

William Howard Taft (second from left) walks with friends on the golf course. Taft, like many other Republicans, saw early the importance of rewarding party activists in the Sunshine State. The state played a major rule in both his 1908 election and 1912 re-nomination. A web of Republicans across the South used the strength of the national party to prosper in the patronage system. (AC.)

Future president Franklin D. Roosevelt (right) is pictured during his tenure as deputy secretary of the Navy. He would run on the 1920 democratic ticket as the party's nominee for vice president. Despite being overwhelmed in that year's election, the entire South was easily won by the Democrats. The state of Florida would play an important role in the Roosevelt New Deal to come. (AC.)

Florida has never produced a native son presidential or vice-presidential nominee. There are several reasons to explain this odd fact. Until World War II, it was the least populous state in the South and failed to produce notable leaders. After the war, Florida politicians in the state were staunch segregationists and held no appeal for the national Democratic Party. (LC.)

Florida has been a home away from home for countless presidents. But in the case of Kennedy and Nixon, it was the location of true presidential residences. Florida was a place they could go and surround themselves with family, to reclaim some of the ordinary life that they had lost due to White House life. (LC.)

Future president Johnson (second from left) and President Kennedy (center) look on as a detailed report is presented by officials at NASA. Florida has also been a hotbed for important presidential decisions and the site of historical change. From the space race to the events of September 11, 2001, Florida has played a central role in the history of the American presidency. (LC.)

Pres. George W. Bush greets sailors and their families at Naval Station Mayport. Over the past few decades, the Bush family and the state of Florida have been closely linked. Press. George H.W. Bush trained here during World War II, and son Jeb was governor of the state, with family members being frequent fixtures in the state capitol. (White House.)

President and First Lady Obama arrive in Homestead outside of Homestead Air Force Base. The Sunshine State was critical to the victories of both George W. Bush and Barack Obama. During Bush's victory in 2000, the prolonged statewide recount transformed Tallahassee into the political capital of the world. Since leaving office, both presidents have kept a low profile, yet it is front-page news across Florida whenever they are in town. (White House.)

President Obama acknowledges the crowd during a grassroots event at McArthur High School in Hollywood on November 4, 2012. In early 2017, Obama made news when it was confirmed that he would travel to Florida for a private wedding. The groom was White House staffer and travel director Marvin Nicholson, and the bride was Helen Pajcic, the daughter of Steve Pajcic, a local lawyer who first hosted Obama in March 2007 for a fundraiser at his Avondale home. Steve Pajcic was also a longtime member of the Florida House of Representatives and the Democratic gubernatorial nominee in 1986. Helen was born 15 days after her father's failed bid. This was Obama's last trip to Florida as president. (White House.)

"Florida Sunrise" by Martin Johnson Heade captures the impression most visitors have of the Sunshine State: endless natural beauty under an expanse of sunlight. To define the state of Florida is difficult. But, as this book has demonstrated, all Americans, from all walks of life, including those at the highest pinnacle of power, have been beguiled by Florida. This has resulted in concentrated efforts to preserve the state's natural beauty, as was the case when the state's Everglades were made a national park by President Truman. During the usually destructive development of Florida, the tenacious methods of Teddy Roosevelt saw the creation of Ocala National Forest and the Pelican Island preservation. Other presidents have governed it, fought battles across it, and negotiated for it from the Spanish. Florida is the largest state never to produce an American president, yet it has captivated all American presidents across the centuries. (State Library and Archives of Florida.)

Index of Presidents

About the Truman Little White House

The Harry S. Truman Little White House is Florida's only presidential national historic site.

Constructed in 1890 as naval officer housing, important visitors have included extended stays by inventor Thomas Edison and scientist Edward Hayden, and it has been used by six American presidents. Its most important period was as the winter White House of Harry Truman, who spent 175 days of his presidency here from 1946 through 1952. Truman faced the rebuilding of Europe, the Palestine question, issues of civil rights and labor unrest, changes in foreign policy, and the response to the Cold War here.

Other presidential visitors have included William Howard Taft in 1912, Dwight Eisenhower in 1955–1956, John F. Kennedy in 1961 and 1962, and former presidents Jimmy Carter in 1996 and 2007 and Bill Clinton in 2005. It was the site of international peace talks between the presidents of Armenia and Azerbaijan in 2001.

Open daily, it is the perfect site for any lover of presidential history.